NEW LIFE ...
Jesus

MELISSA C. DOWNEY AND SUSAN L. LINGO

PAGE DESIGN AND ILLUSTRATION BY ROY GREEN

COVER ILLUSTRATION BY TERRI STEIGER

STANDARD
PUBLISHING
Cincinnati, Ohio

Library of Congress Catalog Card Number 93-85775

ISBN 0-7847-0143-1

Copyright © 1994 by Melissa C. Downey, Susan L. Lingo
Published by The STANDARD PUBLISHING Company, Cincinnati, Ohio.
Division of STANDEX INTERNATIONAL Corporation. Printed in U.S.A.

New Life in Jesus

New life in Jesus begins with God's awesome love for us. God sent His only Son, Jesus, to show us His love. A sacrifice had to be made for all the sins of the world, and Jesus' life was that sacrifice. When all the sins were paid for, all sinners could be forgiven and have a new life. So, Jesus died to give us new life.

Jesus knew God's plan. He knew He would die in Jerusalem. But Jesus loves God with His whole heart and always chooses to obey God. So when God sent Jesus to Jerusalem, Jesus obeyed. He had already taught His disciples that He would suffer many things and not be accepted by the Jewish leaders. He had told them that He would be killed and would rise from the dead on the third day after He was killed (Mark 8:31).

Jesus rode a donkey into Jerusalem on the first day of the week. Crowds of people spread palm branches and coats on the road to honor Him. The people shouted "Praise God! God bless the One who comes in the name of the Lord!" (Mark 11:7-9)

The next day, Jesus went to the temple. This was a holy place where people came to worship God. But Jesus found men there who loved money more than they loved God. The men who exchanged foreign money for the temple money overcharged for their service. The men selling lambs and doves for sacrifices also cheated the people. When Jesus saw this, He became very angry. He said, "It is written in the Scriptures, 'My Temple will be a house where people from all nations will pray.' But you are changing God's house into a 'hideout for robbers.'" Jesus threw out the bad men and turned the animals loose (Mark 11:15-17). The Jewish leaders who made a lot of money from the money changers and animal sellers were furious! Not only had Jesus cost them money, but people were following Jesus and listening to Him instead of them! The decided that they had to get rid of Jesus.

On Thursday, Jesus and His disciples shared their last supper together. Jesus told them once again that He was going away, and He told them to

remember Him whenever they shared the wine and the bread together. After the meal, Jesus took a towel and large bowl of water and washed His disciples' feet. He did this to show His love for them and to teach them the importance of serving each other. One of the disciples, Judas, left the meal early to go tell the Jewish leaders where they could find Jesus. The leaders paid Judas thirty pieces of silver because he gave them this information (John 13:1-30).

Later that night, Jesus and the rest of His disciples walked to the Garden of Gethsemane. Jesus wanted to spend time praying because He needed strength from His heavenly Father. Jesus knew that the men who wanted to kill Him would be coming soon. He knew the next hours would be very hard. His choice to obey His heavenly Father was a tough one. Yet, He chose to die to bring us new life. With tears, Jesus prayed for himself, the disciples, and for you! (John 17:20, 21)

When He finished praying, Jesus met the Roman soldiers as they entered the garden. Judas had brought them to Jesus. The soldiers arrested Jesus and took Him to the house of Caiaphas, the Jewish high priest. From there, He was sent to Herod, the Roman ruler of Galilee. Herod sent Jesus to Pilate, the Roman Governor. Pilate did not know what to do with Jesus. Pilate saw nothing wrong with Jesus, yet the Jewish leaders demanded that Jesus be punished (Mark 14:43—15:5).

A large crowd had gathered around Pilate's palace. Pilate asked the crowd what they wanted to happen to Jesus. They shouted, "Crucify Him!" Sadly, Pilate sent Jesus to the cross to die.

When Jesus was dead, friends buried Him in a tomb. Roman soldiers rolled a large stone over the doorway and stood guard to make sure that no one tried to take the body. But just as Jesus promised, on the third day after His death, He rose from the dead (Mark 15:6—16:1-7).

Not long after this, Jesus came to the disciples as they were fishing. Together they shared a breakfast of fish. Later, Jesus led the disciples to a mountainside. There, He told them to go and teach all people about Him and the new life they could receive through Him. Jesus promised that His spirit would always be with them. Then Jesus was carried up to Heaven. The disciples worshiped Jesus, and began to go all over the world to tell others the good news about new life in Jesus (John 21:1-14; Mark 16:14-19).

Message Memory Match

More than 1000 years before Jesus was born, God's men were writing about Him. These special men of God are called prophets. God gives messages to His prophets, and they give God's message to His people. These messages from God are called prophecies. In this way, God lets His people know what is going to happen before it happens.

Most of the prophecies concerning Jesus—the Messiah—were written down in what came to be known as the Old Testament. Then, when the prophecies came true, those events were recorded in what we call the New Testament.

In this game, you will match the Old Testament prophecy about Jesus with the New Testament Scripture that tells about that prophecy being fulfilled. To play the game, cut out the cards. Read the cards, then place them face down on a flat surface. The first child will turn over two cards. If the two match, the child keeps the cards. If not, the cards are turned over again in the same place where they were and the next child takes a turn. The child with the most cards wins.

 "The days are coming," says the Lord, "when I will raise up a good descendant in David's family. This descendant will be a king who will rule in a wise way. . . . In his time Judah will be saved."

Jeremiah 23:5, 6

 This is the family history of Jesus Christ. He came from the family of David.

Matthew 1:1

 "But you, Bethlehem Ephrathah, are one of the smallest towns in Judah. But from you will come one who will rule Israel for me."

Micah 5:2

 Jesus was born in the town of Bethlehem in Judea during the time when Herod was king.

Matthew 2:1

The Spirit of the Lord will rest upon that king. The Spirit gives him wisdom, understanding, guidance and power.

Isaiah 11:2

The little child began to grow up. He became stronger and wiser, and God's blessings were with him.

Luke 2:40

Rejoice, people of Jerusalem. Shout for joy, people of Jerusalem. Your king is coming to you. He does what is right, and he saves. He is gentle and riding on a donkey.

Zechariah 9:9

They took branches of palm trees and went out to meet Jesus. They shouted, "Praise God! God bless the One who comes in the name of the Lord!" Jesus found a colt and sat on it.

John 12:13, 14

He was beaten down and punished. But he didn't say a word. He was like a lamb being led to be killed. . . . He never opened his mouth.

Isaiah 53:7

Then the high priest stood up and said to Jesus, "Aren't you going to answer? Don't you have something to say about their charges against you?" But Jesus said nothing.

Matthew 26:62

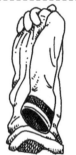
They divided my clothes among them, and they threw lots for my clothing.

Psalm 22:18

After the soldiers nailed Jesus to the cross, they took his clothes. They divided them into four parts. Each soldier got one part.

John 19:23

But the Lord himself will give you a sign: The virgin will be pregnant. She will have a son.

Isaiah 7:14

God sent the angel Gabriel to a virgin who lived in Nazareth. . . . The angel said to her, "Listen! You will become pregnant. You will give birth to a son."

Luke 1:26-31

My best and truest friend ate at my table. Now even he has turned against me.

Psalm 41:9

One of the 12 followers, Judas Iscariot, went to talk to the leading priests. Judas offered to give Jesus to them.

Mark 14:10

Palm Sunday

PALM SUNDAY bursts into our lives in the springtime when NEW LIFE is blossoming from flower buds and tiny green leaves, and baby animals are born! Palm Sunday is the beginning of our celebration of Jesus' victory over death. Palm Sunday is the Sunday before Easter and was the day Jesus came into the city of Jerusalem for the last time.

The name "Palm Sunday" comes from the palm leaves that were scattered over Jesus' path on His way into Jerusalem. As Jesus came near the city, His followers sang praise songs to Him and scattered palm leaves along the path. Palm leaves and branches were the symbols for VICTORY.

The celebration of Palm Sunday is a special time for us to remember how Jesus came to Jerusalem to die for us and to bring us the **victory** of forgiveness and **new life** with God! Five days after Palm Sunday, Jesus died on a cross to pay the price for our sins!

As we welcome Jesus into our lives, we may sing praises to Him just as the crowds outside of Jerusalem sang when they saw Jesus coming towards them! What words can we sing to Jesus? Find all of the letters in each set of shapes. Unscramble them and write them in the blank spaces to find the words of praise Jesus' followers shouted on that first Palm Sunday!

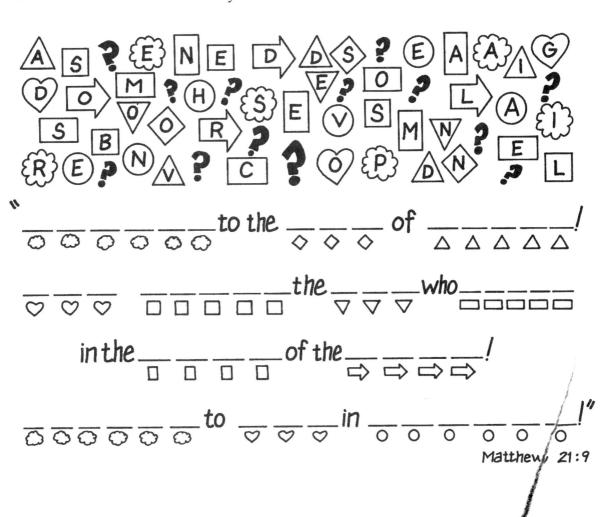

Matthew 21:9

It's a Date

Travel to countries in warm parts of the world and you
7

are likely to see the beauty and grace of the palm tree.
15   3

In Galilee and Judea where Jesus lived, palm trees covered
1   19

the countryside.
20

There are many types of palm trees, but the date palm was
8

the most important one in Bible times because the entire tree was used
18

in one way or another to provide for God's people. Its fruit, the date,
16   10   5

was food for the Hebrews and provided them with the mineral iron for
12

energy. Raw, cooked, and baked into breads, dates were a daily treat!
11

The sap from the date palm was used to make wine, and the date seeds
14

were ground to make food for camels. Leaf stems were woven into rope
2

and the tall, sturdy trunk of the date palm tree was used to build ladders,
9

carts, and houses. Smaller parts of the trunk were used for spoons and tools.
4

Modern people who live where Jesus lived still rely on the date palm just
13

like the people in Jesus' day. God has given us this mighty, royal tree to feed,
17

protect, and shelter us, as well as to give us shade and beauty. When you think of
6

it, Jesus is like the palm tree!

Use the numbered letters above to fill in the Scripture verse below.

<u> </u> <u> </u>   <u> </u> <u> </u> <u> </u>   <u> </u> <u> </u> <u> </u> <u> </u>   <u> </u> <u> </u> <u> </u> <u> </u>   <u> </u> <u> </u> <u> </u> <u> </u> <u> </u> ,   <u> </u> <u> </u> <u> </u>
1 2   3 4 5   6 7 8 9   10 4 4 11   2 12 5 1 9 ,   3 4 5

<u> </u> <u> </u> <u> </u> <u> </u>   <u> </u> <u> </u> <u> </u> <u> </u>   <u> </u> <u> </u> <u> </u>   <u> </u> <u> </u> <u> </u> <u> </u>   <u> </u> <u> </u> <u> </u> <u> </u> . <u> </u>
13 5 14 9   13 7 15 16   9 17 16   9 12 16 16   10 4 4 11 .   7

<u> </u> <u> </u> <u> </u> <u> </u>   <u> </u> <u> </u>   <u> </u> <u> </u> <u> </u> <u> </u>   <u> </u> <u> </u>   <u> </u> <u> </u> <u> </u>   <u> </u> <u> </u> <u> </u> <u> </u>
9 12 16 16   1 14   15 8 4 6 8   18 3   9 17 16   15 1 8 11

<u> </u> <u> </u>   <u> </u> <u> </u> <u> </u> <u> </u>   <u> </u> <u> </u>   <u> </u> <u> </u> <u> </u> <u> </u> <u> </u> <u> </u> <u> </u> .
4 2   2 12 5 1 9   1 9   19 12 4 11 5 20 16 14 .

Matthew 12:33

The Lord's Palm

The Lord gives us the date palm, the royal palm and the coconut palm — but the greatest palm He gives to us is the palm of His own loving hand! The Lord stretches out His hands to help us. He stretches out His hands to lovingly invite us to follow Him and to serve Him. The Lord even stretched out His hands to die for us! Jesus' hands were nailed to a cross in the greatest act of love there has ever been! Because Jesus loved us so much, He gave His life so we could live with God!

The Bible tells us that there is something else very special about the palms of the Lord's hands. The Bible says that *YOUR OWN NAME* is written upon the palm of God's own loving hand!

Make the **LORD'S PALM TREE** by tracing your own hand on green construction paper and *carefully* cutting it out. Glue a red heart in the center of His palm and write your name upon it. Then color the palm trunk on this page, cut it out, and glue the Lord's Palm to the trunk! (You may wish to slightly bend the fingers to give the "palm leaves" a more graceful look!)

See, I have written your name on my hand.   Isaiah 49:16

Money Changing

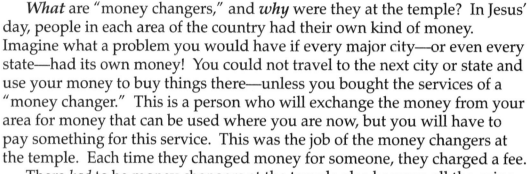

What are "money changers," and *why* were they at the temple? In Jesus' day, people in each area of the country had their own kind of money. Imagine what a problem you would have if every major city—or even every state—had its own money! You could not travel to the next city or state and use your money to buy things there—unless you bought the services of a "money changer." This is a person who will exchange the money from your area for money that can be used where you are now, but you will have to pay something for this service. This was the job of the money changers at the temple. Each time they changed money for someone, they charged a fee.

There *had* to be money changers at the temple also because all the coins from all the different places had pictures of important people stamped on them and these kinds of coins were considered unholy. Only coins stamped with the coins' value could be used in the temple.

If the money changers at the temple were necessary, why did Jesus get angry when He saw them? Because they were charging too much and cheating the people who had come to worship God. Not all the money changers were bad, but the dishonest ones caused Jesus to be angry.

Jesus' anger came from His love for the people. He didn't like cheating. His anger also came from His love for His Father's house, the temple. The temple was a holy place where the people came to worship and praise God, and show their love for Him. This is why Jesus ran the money changers out of the temple courtyard.

In the following activity, you can practice changing money.
We'll pretend that $1 = 1 talent
                              25¢ = 1 shekel
                              5¢ = 5 mites

The cost of the exchange is 35¢. The money changer may charge this in American money or in Bible-times money.

Give each child a column of money to color and cut out. Then select one child to be the money changer and give all the talents, shekels, and mites to the money changer. Every other child will be left with $1, 2 50¢ pieces, 4 quarters and 2 nickels. After all the children have exchanged their money, add up the amount the money changer has made.

Teachers and parents may wish to have items available for sale; balloons, candy, etc. with Bible-times price tags!

The Bread of Life

The night before Jesus died on the cross, He ate His last supper with the twelve disciples. The LAST SUPPER was a very important supper! Jesus took bread and wine and shared it with His friends. He told them the bread was like His body and the wine was like His blood. Jesus was *sharing His whole being* with the people who loved Him! He told His disciples that they should share the bread and the wine as a way of remembering Him. This special celebration of sharing Jesus' body and blood is called, "COMMUNION."

Christian churches all over the world share the service of Communion. When we drink the juice and eat the bread, we remember how Jesus gave His life for us. Communion reminds us of the love and life we share with Jesus. And as we eat the bread and drink the cup, we are telling Jesus we accept Him **into our lives** every day!

This is why Jesus is **THE BREAD OF LIFE!** Like earthly bread that gives life to our bodies, Jesus is the spiritual bread that gives life to our eternal spirits.

Make a loaf of SCRIPTURE BREAD to remind you of the NEW LIFE we have in Jesus! Each ingredient is found in a Scripture verse. To get cookin', use your Bible to find each ingredient and write it in the blank space.

Pre-heat oven to 325 degrees. Grease a loaf pan.

¾ cup Jeremiah 6:20 _____

1 Jeremiah 17:11 _____

½ cup Psalm 55:21 _____

Mix in large bowl.

Pour dough into pan. Bake in Leviticus 2:4 _____ for 25 minutes.

1½ cup Leviticus 6:15 _____

½ teaspoon Matthew 5:13 _____

2 teaspoons Proverbs 7:17 _____

Mix well, add to above.

After you Luke 22:19 _____, the Lord for your bread,

½ cup Song of Solomon 6:11, chopped _____

1 cup Proverbs 25:11, chopped _____

¾ cup 1 Samuel 30:12 _____

Mix into dough.

Eat and Enjoy

The Leader Should Be Like The Servant

"I am more important than you are! I should be first!"

Have you ever heard this? Have you ever said this? Jesus heard the disciples arguing during their last supper together. Each one thought that he was more important to Jesus than the others.

Jesus said to them, "The kings of the world rule over their people. Men who have authority over others are called, 'very important.' But you must not be like that. The greatest among you should be like the youngest, and the leader should be like the servant" (Luke 22:25, 26).

Then Jesus, the Lord of Heaven and earth, showed the disciples what He meant. He took a bowl of water and a towel and one by one, He washed their feet. Imagine! The Son of God washing dirty feet! Usually, only lowly servants did such a job! But, by doing this, Jesus showed the disciples how a leader can choose to be a giving servant.

Jesus was teaching the disciples and us to choose to be Givers instead of getters. Jesus wants us to be Givers. Living the new life in Jesus means choosing to serve and to be last. The most interesting thing about this is that it often takes more courage and more strength to be a Giver, than to be a getter. A getter demands to be first, to get his or her own way, but a Giver is BIG enough to think, "I don't need to be first," or, "I'd like to make you happy by giving you the biggest piece."

Place a big G by the things a Giver would say and a little g by the things a getter would say.

_____ That's mine and you can't use it!

_____ You take the first turn.

_____ I get to ride in the front seat! I called it first.

_____ I'll help you with that.

_____ Lynn should go first. She's great at this game.

_____ I'm not going to clean up that mess. I wasn't the only one at that table!

Pressed in Prayer

On the night before Jesus died, He went to an olive garden to pray. Heavy, heavy problems were pressing on Jesus' heart, and He prayed a very powerful prayer. Oddly enough, the name of the garden where Jesus prayed means "oil press." In an oil press, heavy stones are placed on olives (or other fruit) to squeeze out the oil or juice. Just as the heavy stones press on olives, the sins of all the world pressed on Jesus as He prayed. The sins of the world squeezed Jesus' heart and Jesus *poured out His love* in a prayer to God!

In the puzzle below, use the paragraph above and John 17:21-23 to help fill in the missing words. You will find out about Jesus' prayer and the name of the garden will be squeezed in the center!

In the ◯ _ _ _ _ _ _ Jesus

_ _ _ _ _ _ ◯ _ to His Father:

"I pray ◯ _ _ _

_ _ _ _ _ ◯ people can also

be one in _ ◯ so that the world

will _ _ _ _ _ _ _ ◯ that you

sent ◯ _ . I will be in

them ◯ _ _ you will

be _ ◯ _

_ ◯ _ ."

Prayer: Talking with God

How do we talk with God?
Does it matter if we fold our hands?
Or if we sit or stand?
Do we have to sound serious?
Or be mysterious?

What matters is our heart.
    (Jeremiah 29:13)
We must be open and honest, ready to obey.
    (2 Chronicles 7:14)
We can talk with God this way.
Because He know us and before we say a word,
We can know that God has already heard.
    (Isaiah 65:24)

Jesus talked with His heavenly Father often (Luke 5:16). How often is often? Use your Bible to look up the verses below. Then match the verses with the statements.

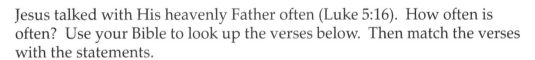

John 11:38-42	Jesus prayed in the morning.
Mark 1:35	Jesus prayed at night.
Luke 9:18	Jesus prayed when alone.
Luke 6:12	Jesus prayed in public.

When people tell us about things from the Bible, we can always "**check it out!**" Look up the verses in the poem above and see what you can learn about prayer.

The Cost of Forgiveness

What is the cost of forgiveness? Why do we need to be forgiven? Whenever we do something that God said not to do, or when we do not do what God said to do, we are sinning. Sin makes our hearts dirty and keeps us from God.

Before Jesus, the way to receive forgiveness was to offer a sacrifice to God. The only sacrifice that was acceptable to God in payment for sin was a perfect lamb. The priests would kill the lamb on an altar and then it would be burned as a way of sending it up to God.

Why did this have to be? "The law (of God) says that almost everything must be made clean by blood. And sins cannot be forgiven without blood to show death" (Hebrews 9:22).

Jesus came to be our perfect lamb. Because He is the Son of God, His life was perfect. God gave Jesus as the perfect sacrifice. His death paid for all sins, for all time.

"Look, the Lamb of God. He takes away the sins of the world!" (John 1:29)

"All people have sinned and are not good enough for God's glory. People are made right with God by his grace, which is a free gift. They are made right with God by being made free from sin through Jesus Christ. God gave Jesus as a way to forgive sin through faith. And all of this is because of the blood of Jesus' death" (Romans 3:23-25).

What is the cost of forgiveness? Why did God pay the price?

Use your Bible to look up 1 John 4:9, 10 to fill in the blanks below. Then you will have the answer to these questions.

This is how _____ showed his _____ to us: He sent his _____ _____ into the world to _____ us _____ through him. True _____ is _____ love for _____, not _____ love for _____. God sent his _____ to be the _____ to take _____ our sins.

Why Did Jesus Have to Die?

Jesus came to die for us, but WHY?

Each of us has done many wrong things. We have said mean things to others, we have been jealous, or hateful, we have lied, we have disobeyed our parents. We have ALL sinned. And although God loves each of us, He does not accept our sins! We cannot do anything to make up for our sins, but Jesus can and DID! Jesus *died* to pay for our sins and because He did, our sins are forgiven! Jesus came to die for us so that we could be God's friends again. Jesus came to die for us so we can *live forever with God!*

Oh, Father God, in Heaven high,
Why did Jesus have to die?
He came in love, Your only Son
To teach us that Your will be done.

With miracles He cured the blind
And healed disease of every kind.
He taught your truth for every ear
But stubborn ones chose not to hear.

These were the few who said He'd lied;
They threw His life and love aside!
And even when my Jesus rose,
They were as cold as winter snows.

So, Father, though it makes me cry,
I know why Jesus had to die—

So I can live with you!

Cut out the puzzle pieces below and glue them onto a piece of paper to find a prayer you can pray to thank God for sending Jesus to love you and die for your sins.

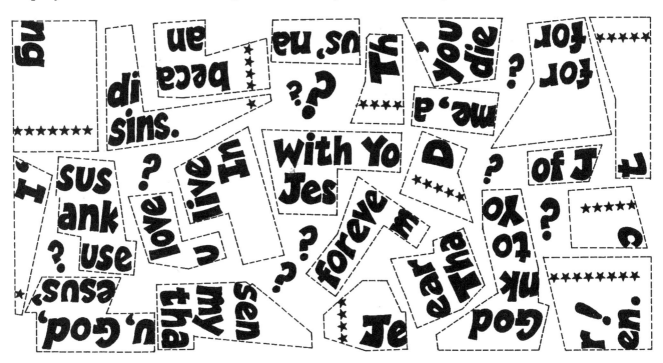

Choices

Do you know that Jesus **chose** to die on the cross? He didn't have to. The Bible says He could have called down armies of angels to save Him (Matthew 26:53). He could have used His own awesome power to hurt the people who hurt Him. Instead, He chose to show his love for us.

This was not an easy choice for Jesus to make. He knew how much it would hurt His body and His heart. That is why He asked His Father if there could be another way (Matthew 26:39). But there was no other way, and so Jesus chose to obey His heavenly Father. He **chose** to bring us new life.

You make choices too. Sometimes it is difficult to make the right choice—to do the right thing. Play this game with a few friends to think about some of the choices you have to make.

Needed: The game board
A file folder
Game pieces for each player
Game situation cards
One die

Directions: Make copies of the game board, the situation cards, and the player pieces (as many as needed). Mount the game board to the inside of the file folder for easy storage. Cut out the player pieces and the cards. These may be laminated for longer life.

To play the game: Roll the die to see who goes first. Player 1 draws a card and reads (adult may read) the situation. Player 1 decides between the choices. If he chooses to do the right thing, he may roll the die and advance that number of spaces. If he chooses to do a wrong thing, he will go back 2 spaces. Players may discuss the choices to decide which is right or wrong.

If a player lands on "Stuck in the Muck," she will be stuck for one turn.

If a player lands on "Good Choice" or "Bad Choice," she will advance or retreat one space accordingly.

The first player to reach or pass "Home" wins.

At lunch, you find 75¢ on the table. You decide to:

A. Put it in your pocket.
B. Turn it in to the office.

You are at the mall with a friend. Your friend dares you to steal something. You decide to:

A. Take the dare.
B. Refuse to do it.

The school bully calls you a bad name. You decide to:

A. Ignore him.
B. Call him a bad name.

You are at home and can't find your money. After looking for a few minutes, you decide to:

A. Ask for help.
B. Storm out of your room shouting, "Someone stole my money!"

You didn't study for a spelling test. The person next to you usually makes 100's. You decide to:

A. Look at his paper to make sure you do well.
B. Do the best you can by yourself.

You just got a new bike. Your parent says you may ride up to 2 blocks away. There is an awesome hill 4 blocks away. You decide to:

A. Go ride the hill.
B. Ask your parent about riding the hill.

Your little brother or sister is driving you crazy. You decide to:

A. Yell and sock him/her.
B. Try to be patient, remembering that you were little once, too.

You are having a party for your class. But there is one person in your class you do not want to invite. You decide to:

A. Invite everyone.
B. Invite everyone except the one you don't like.

You and your friend are playing catch and you break a window. You decide to:

A. Confess quickly.
B. Blame your friend for breaking it.
C. Pretend to know nothing about it.

You are watching TV at a friend's house. Your friend wants to watch a show you are not allowed to watch. You decide to:

A. Say nothing and watch the program.
B. Ask your friend to change programs.
C. Go home.

A new neighbor moves to your street. He is from another country. You chose to:

A. Make fun of him because he is different.
B. Ask him about his country and tell him about yours.

Your friend Sam want you to come over when his parents are away. When you ask to go, you decide to:

A. Tell your parent the truth.
B. Tell your parent Sam's parents will be home.

You are in the grocery store. Candy samples are 5¢ each. You don't have 5¢. You decide to:

A. Wait until you have the money.
B. Take one anyway; no one will notice.

Your friend Mary said something bad about you to John. John told you what she said. You decide to:

A. Go to Mary and ask her about it.
B. Tell everyone that Mary is no longer your friend.

The teacher left the room. The class bully breaks the treat jar. Then he says he will beat up anyone who tells. When asked you decide to:

A. Say, "I don't know."
B. Tell the truth.
C. Say, "We all know who did it, but are afraid to tell."

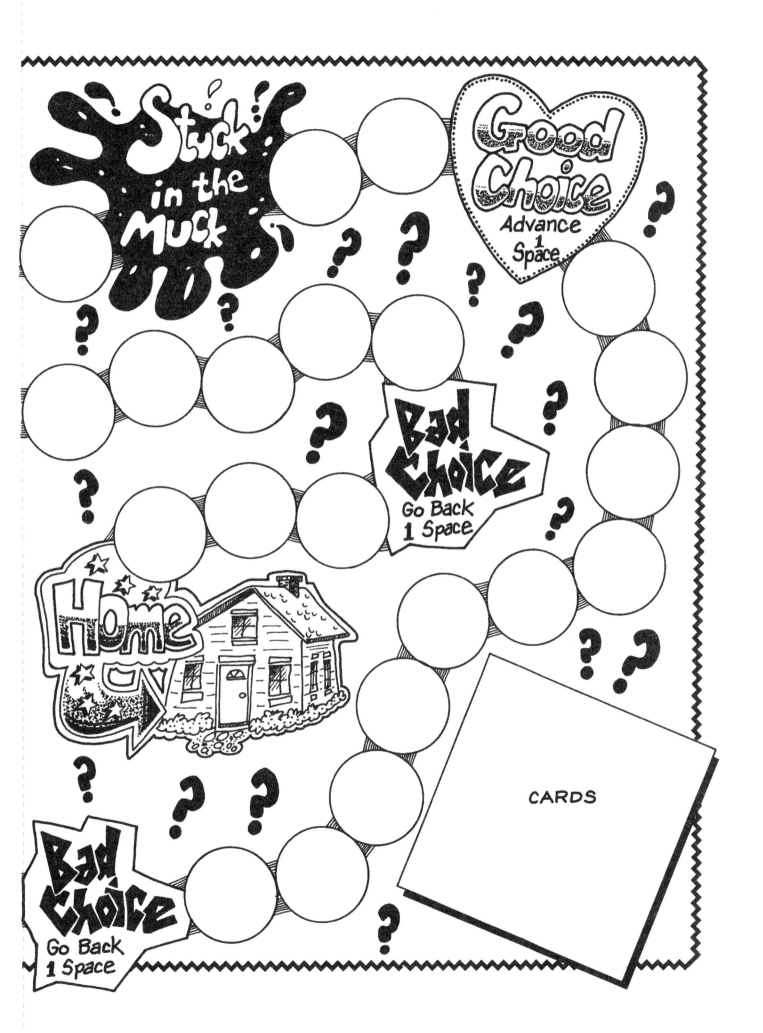

Guard That Tomb!

In Jesus' day the tombs (burial places) were natural or man-made caves. The doorway of the man-made tomb was about four feet high. The inside was about five feet high. Joseph of Arimathea took the body of Jesus down from the cross and placed it in a tomb that he had made (Matthew 27:57-60). Then he covered the door to Jesus' tomb with a stone that weighed 1½ to 2 tons. That is as much as two or three school vans!

Pilate placed his official seal across the door. The seal was a rope stretched across the stone and held in place on either side by a large patch of wax. The wax was melted over the rope, and then a Roman seal was pressed in the soft wax. If the rope was moved, the seal would be broken. In this way, anyone could tell if the stone had been disturbed.

Pilate also ordered Roman soldiers to guard Jesus' tomb. Roman soldiers were famous for their strength and courage. No fewer than sixteen men made up a guard unit. Four men were on duty at all times. They followed orders well because if a soldier did not follow orders, he was severely punished—or killed!

Why was Pilate so worried about guarding the place where Jesus was buried? Pilate knew that Jesus had said that He would rise from the dead. The soldiers were to make sure that no one stole Jesus' body to make it *look* like Jesus had risen from the dead. So, when Jesus *did* rise from the dead, the soldiers were afraid that they would be punished for failing to do their job. But instead of being punished, the soldiers were given money to lie and say that the disciples stole Jesus' body.

Think About It!

Why did Pilate want his soldiers to say the body had been stolen?
Who moved the heavy stone away?
Could anyone or anything have stopped the power of God?

Read more about the Resurrection of Jesus in Matthew 28, Mark 16, Luke 24, and John 20.

Read all about it!

If there had been newspapers in Jesus' day, what do you think the headlines would have read when Jesus came back to life? Read the articles from the *Gospel Times* below and then match each article to the Bible references at the bottom of the page. Write the reference on the line under each news item.

The Gospel Times

Today's Weather: The Light shines in the darkness. And the darkness has not overpowered the Light.

"This is what God told us: God has given us eternal life, and this life is in his Son."

My friend Cleopas and I were on our way to the city of Emmaeus. We were talking about the terrible things that had happened in Jerusalem when a stranger joined us on the road. He asked us what we were talking about and we said that he must have been the only person in Jerusalem not to know that the prophet, Jesus, had been killed. "We were hoping that He would free the Jews," we said to the stranger. Then the stranger said to us, "You are foolish and slow to realize what is true. You should believe everything the prophets said. They said that the Christ must suffer these things before he enters his glory."

Then the stranger began to explain the holy Scriptures to us more clearly than we had ever heard them explained before! When we reached Emmaeus, the stranger started to go on, but we begged Him to stay and share the evening meal with us. He did, and when He took the bread and gave thanks for it, broke it and gave it to us, we finally realized who He was! This was Jesus! He *was* alive! He *had* risen from the dead!

My name used to be Simon and I was a fisherman with my brother, Andrew. We fished in the Sea of Galilee. One day, Jesus came to us and told us to follow Him and become fishermen for men! I went with Jesus and He changed my name to Peter. "Peter" means "rock," but there was one time in my life when I was not very rock-like. I had traveled with Jesus and knew Him very well. I knew He was the Son of God and yet, when He was arrested and brought to Pilate, I was terrified. I was so afraid that when a servant girl said she had seen me with Jesus, I denied it! I denied that I even knew Him! How could I have done such a thing? After Jesus was killed, I was filled with shame and sorrow! But Jesus came to me! He loves me enough to forgive me for betraying Him, and he came to me to tell me this himself!

"My name is Thomas and I am one of Jesus' disciples. I traveled with Jesus and served Him right up until His horrible death. His death made me sad and sick because I loved Jesus more than anything! After His death, many of His followers met together to pray and share our pain over Jesus' death. Our Jesus was gone forever—or so we thought! All of a sudden, I looked up and there was Jesus, standing before me! I kept thinking, Can this truly be Jesus? Is He really standing here before me? Jesus knew my doubts and He told me to place my fingertips into the nail holes in His hands. I reached out and touched Him and then I was certain that this was really Jesus and He was really alive!

JESUS IS RISEN!

John 20:25-29   1 John 5:11   Luke 24:13-17   Luke 22:56-62   John 1:5

The Road to New Life

Use the story at the beginning of this book to put the events below in order. Number the statements from 1 to 10, in the order that they happened. Then draw lines from each number to the place on the map where that event took place.

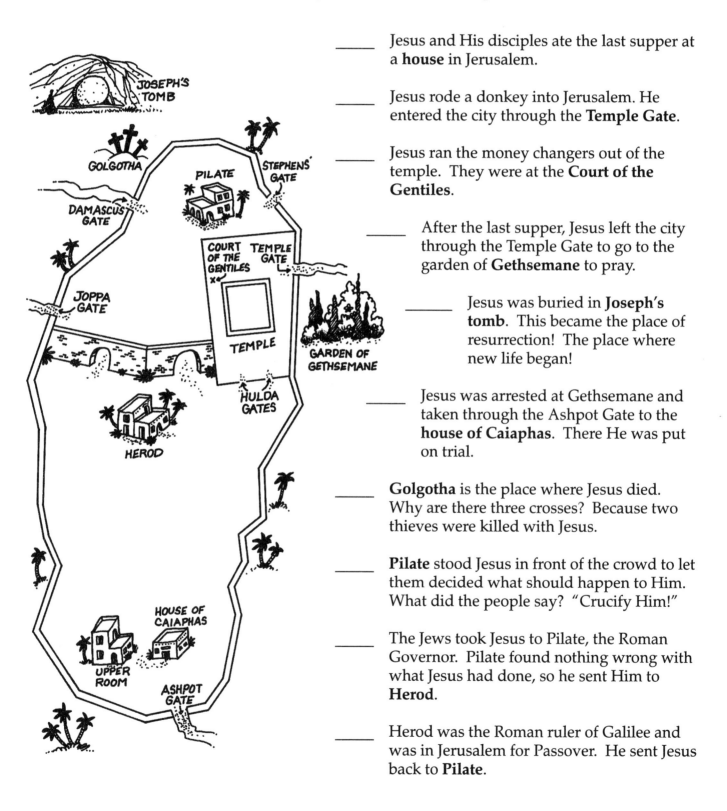

_____ Jesus and His disciples ate the last supper at a **house** in Jerusalem.

_____ Jesus rode a donkey into Jerusalem. He entered the city through the **Temple Gate**.

_____ Jesus ran the money changers out of the temple. They were at the **Court of the Gentiles**.

_____ After the last supper, Jesus left the city through the Temple Gate to go to the garden of **Gethsemane** to pray.

_____ Jesus was buried in **Joseph's tomb**. This became the place of resurrection! The place where new life began!

_____ Jesus was arrested at Gethsemane and taken through the Ashpot Gate to the **house of Caiaphas**. There He was put on trial.

_____ **Golgotha** is the place where Jesus died. Why are there three crosses? Because two thieves were killed with Jesus.

_____ **Pilate** stood Jesus in front of the crowd to let them decided what should happen to Him. What did the people say? "Crucify Him!"

_____ The Jews took Jesus to Pilate, the Roman Governor. Pilate found nothing wrong with what Jesus had done, so he sent Him to **Herod**.

_____ Herod was the Roman ruler of Galilee and was in Jerusalem for Passover. He sent Jesus back to **Pilate**.

The Bridge

Like a bridge leads us safely across rough waters to a safe and beautiful land, Jesus leads us from sin and temptation in this life to our holy Father in Heaven!

Jesus is a bridge from God to man, from hate in this world to love in the next, from the darkness of sin to the light of the Lord!

Try to solve these word bridges! Begin with the word at the top of the bridge. Using the clues and changing only the letter in the box, place the new word in each space.

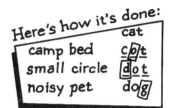

Here's how it's done:
	cat
camp bed	c[o]t
small circle	[d]ot
noisy pet	do[g]

DARK

morning bird [ ]———

type of fat ———[ ]

L[O]RD

HATE

to own ——[ ]—

where a bear naps [ ]———

a bay ———[ ]—

[L]OVE

GOD

peas grow in this [ ]——

cushion ——[ ]—

angry [ ]——

MA[N]

The Seed Cycle

God, our heavenly Father, teaches us through the world He created. With something as small as a seed, He teaches us about new life in Jesus.

During the spring and summer, plants make seeds. In the fall, the plants die. The seeds fall to the ground and are buried in the soil during the winter. As the warmth of spring comes, the seeds grow into new, strong plants. Just as Jesus died, the plants die. But, just as Jesus rose from death, the buried seeds grow with new life.

New life in you begins with a seed of faith. This seed of faith is believing in your heart that Jesus is God's Son and that He died on the cross and rose from the dead to bring us new life. Once this seed of faith is planted, it grows strong in the warmth of His love—and we grow to become more like Jesus!

Seeds are wonderfully made! Each seed has a coat (1) to wear as protection until it is time to grow. Inside the seed is a tiny, living plant (2). The seed also stores food (3) for the baby plant to use until it grows strong enough to break the coat and use the soil outside as food.

Use what you learn in the paragraph above to label this seed:

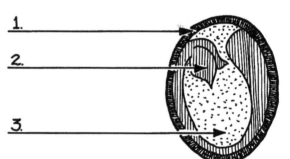

1. _____

2. _____

3. _____

Seed Sorting

Needed: various seeds (peach, apple, nuts, beans, etc.) Sort the seeds by shape, color, size. Notice the great variety that God has created. Talk about the kinds of plants that will grow from each seed. What kinds of seeds do we eat? What kinds of plants have seeds that are almost as big as the fruit?

Seed Planting

Needed: soil, seeds (beans, flowers, vegetable) Styrofoam™ egg carton, toothpicks, paper labels, water

Directions: Put soil in the egg carton. Dampen. Plant seeds by rows in the egg carton and label by using a toothpick stake with a paper label. Keep garden watered but not soaked. Children will check seed growth. Point out the differences in the plants as they sprout.

The Clean Scene

When you are dirty and need a bath, it does no good to wash *only* your knees or *only* your ears—to get really clean, you must let the soap and water cover all of you! The sin in our lives makes us unclean inside and out and no bath will ever clean us enough! Only Jesus can make us truly clean and new and only if we let Jesus wash us inside and out.

The Lord Jesus gave His life to lead us home to Heaven. Because of His death, we are able to stand clean before our heavenly Father. Because of the death of Jesus, our old unclean lives of sin have been washed as clean and white as snow!

Scripture: "God is in the light. . . . And when we live in the light, the blood of the death of Jesus, God's Son, is making us clean from every sin."

1 John 1:7

Make a soap snowball to remind you of how Jesus came to clean us white as snow!

You Need: (for 10 snowballs)
½ box Ivory Snow™ soap flakes
bowl, foil, electric mixer, water

Directions:
1. Pour soap flakes into bowl and add ¾ cup water.
2. Mix, and add a little more water slowly until soap is very stiff. If it gets too sticky, add more soap flakes.
3. Use your hands to form the mixture into golf ball-sized balls and set on foil to dry. (Allow a few days drying time before using.)

Enjoy washing yourself with snow soap!

Scripture Memory

For God loved the world so much that he gave his only Son. God gave his Son so that whoever believes in him may not be lost, but have eternal life.

John 3:16

Jesus is Lord of our lives because God loved the world so much! Make a **"World of Love"** to help you learn one of the most precious Bible verses!

You Need:

1 blue balloon
fishing line or yarn

Directions:

1. Color the hearts below with green and brown (to look like land). Cut them out carefully.

2. Blow up the balloon and glue or tape the hearts around the balloon so that you can read the verse correctly.

3. Hang the balloon with the yarn.

1. "For God loved the world so much that He gave

2. His only Son. God gave

3. His Son so that whoever believes in Him may not

4. be lost, but have eternal life."

John 3:16

Picture This!

Jesus came to us to be our loving PATHWAY to God. He is our SAVIOR, our NEW LIFE and our BEST FRIEND. To help us understand how awesome Jesus is, the writers of the Bible describe Jesus in many different ways. By comparing Jesus to things we can see and understand, we have a better idea of how wonderful Jesus is!

In the puzzle below are a few of the ways Jesus is described in the Bible. Use your Bible to look up each reference and find the missing word in His name below. Then color the pictures, cut them out and glue them into their correct spaces.

1. I am the _____ that gives life (John 6:48).

2. I have come as _____ into the world (John 12:46).

3. I am the true _____ (John 15:1).

4. Look, the _____ of God (John 1:29).

5. I am the _____ (John 10:9).

6. I am the bright morning _____ (Revelation 22:16).

7. The _____ from the tribe of Judah (Revelation 5:5).

8. Thanks be to God for his _____ that is too wonderful to explain (2 Corinthians 9:15).

A Heart in a Heart in a Heart

Jesus has promised that if we are faithful and love Him, He will be in us and we will be in Him! And because of the love of Jesus, *we are all in the Father!*

Make a ♥ in a ♥ in a ♥! Fold a piece of pink or red construction paper in half. Copy the pattern below onto the folded edge of your paper. Cut carefully along the lines to make three hearts. In the smallest heart, write your name. In the next biggest heart write, "Jesus," and in the biggest heart, write, "God, our heavenly Father." Now tape yarn or fishing line behind each heart. Cut out and tape the Scripture verse to the yarn, and then hang your mobile from the ceiling or in a doorway.

**On that day you will know
that I am in my Father.
You will know that you are in me
and I am in you.**

John 14:20

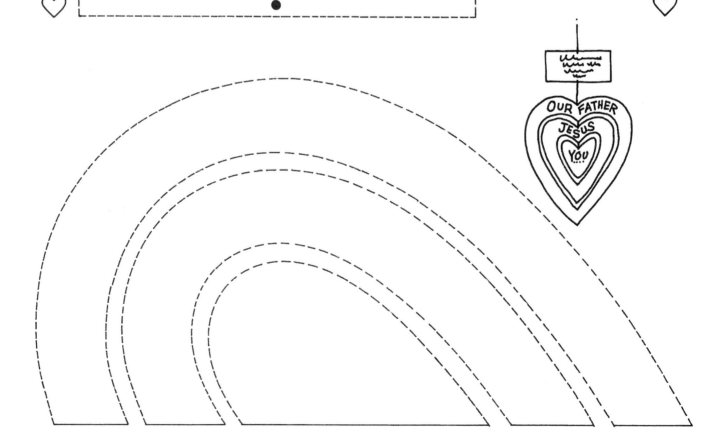

Teach Your World

Jesus told His disciples to go everywhere in the world and tell the good news to everyone. Disciples are people who follow Jesus and learn from Him; are you a disciple? When Jesus said, "Go everywhere in the world," He meant exactly that. As children, we cannot *go everywhere* yet, but we can *tell everyone* in our own world.

Who are the people in your world? These pictures will suggest people to you. Who else is in your world? List the people you can tell about Jesus.

_____   _____

_____   _____

_____   _____

_____   _____

Spreadin' the News!

Before Jesus ascended (rose) to be with our Father in Heaven, He spoke to His disciples. There, on a mountain, Jesus gave His last earthly command! Jesus told the disciples to:

1. Go into the word
2. Baptize people
3. Teach them to obey God's Word
4. Remember that I will be with you always

This beautiful command is called, "the Great Commission," and is meant for *all* of Jesus' disciples! It is very important to know that **WE** are given the awesome responsibility to tell others about Jesus! It is not only our responsibility, but our privilege; we can feel honored that God Almighty chooses to use us to spread His most important message!

In this puzzle are the words to the Great Commission. Travel around the world gathering words to fill in the spaces below. Then unscramble the bold letters to spell what we are spreading to the whole world!

Matthew 28:19, 20

SOGOANDMAKEF**O**LLOWERSOFALLPEOPLEIN**T**HEWORLD.BAPTIZE**T**HEMINTHE**N**AMEOFTHEFATHERANDTHES**O**NANDTHEHOLYSPIRIT.TEACHTHEMTOOBEYEVERYTHIN**G**THATIHAVET**O**LDYOU.YOUCANBESURETHATIWILLBE**W**ITHYOUALWAYS.IWILLCONTINU**E**WITHYOUUNTILTHEEN**D**OFTHEWORLD.

___ ___ ___

___ ___ ___ ___

___ ___ ___ ___ .

___ ___ ___ ___

___ ___ ___ ___

___ ___ ___ ___ .

___ ___ ___ ___

___ ___ ___ .

___ ___ ___ ___ ___ ___ .

___ ___ ___ ___

___ ___ ___ . ___

We're spreading: ___ ___ ___ ___ ___ ___ ___